UNSTABLE
NEIGHBOURHOOD
RABBIT

UNSTABLE NEIGHBOURHOOD RABBIT

MIKKO HARVEY

ANANSI

Published in Canada in 2018 and the USA in 2018
by House of Anansi Press Inc.
www.houseofanansi.com

House of Anansi Press is committed to protecting our natural environment.
As part of our efforts, the interior of this book is printed on paper made from
second-growth forests and is acid-free.

22   21   20   19   18   1   2   3   4   5

Library and Archives Canada Cataloguing in Publication

Harvey, Mikko, author
Unstable neighbourhood rabbit / Mikko Harvey.

Poems.
Issued in print and electronic formats.
ISBN 978-1-4870-0360-9 (softcover).—ISBN 978-1-4870-0361-6
(hardcover).—ISBN 978-1-4870-0362-3 (PDF)

I. Title.

PS8615.A77387U57 2018   C811'.6   C2017-904737-X
C2017-904738-8

Library of Congress Control Number: 2017947366

Book design: Alysia Shewchuk

We acknowledge for their financial support of our publishing program
the Canada Council for the Arts, the Ontario Arts Council, and the Government of Canada
through the Canada Book Fund.

Printed and bound in Canada

CONTENTS

AUTOBIOGRAPHY

The bomb and the raindrop overlap briefly.

Nice night, says the drop.

Where you headed? says the bomb.

Don't know, says the drop.

Well goodbye, says the bomb.

The bomb thinks, *I am too heavy to make friends*. Then he touches the mudbrick building.

Shortly after, landing in debris, the drop thinks, *O*.

BIRD CALL ASSOCIATION

Andre got up and gave a crow call, the same one
he gave every year — well, maybe a little sharper
this time around, but still not enough
to take the cake, so he sat down.

Thirteen of us sat in a circle. Sat in a circle
of metallic chairs in the Gamemaster's basement.

Jessica, a newcomer, tried a hawk call.
Sit down, Jessica, you have much to learn,
was the general unspoken feeling. And so she did.

There was Jon with his overeager chickadee
and Desiree with her competent but lifeless oriole,
both sitting down in turn.

Then Martin, the mailman, surprised everyone
with a barred owl call. The Association
looked at itself nervously. This was the first time
someone had brought an owl call to the circle.
But — the general unspoken conclusion was —
no harm done, and in fact, thank you Martin,
this was nice, but sit down now, because nice
is not enough. And so he did.

Next up was the one we used to call Sarah
before she became a Burning Wing. She sang
a black-and-white warbler, utterly clearly.
She sang it again. Her face looked calm.
You could tell she already knew her fate.

She sang it again. The Association rose to its feet.
She sang it again. An ecstasy spread
through the room like a gust of wind.
And she never stopped singing it—
not when we lifted her onto our shoulders, chanting,
not when we carried her through the shadowy hallways,
not when we peeled off her clothing, everybody wanting
to touch the sublime, not even when we slid her bare body
into the tub full of gasoline and the Gamemaster struck
and dropped a single match, declaring: *Burning Wing.*

SWIVEL

When I want to be sweet and light like a blackberry
floating in a bowl of water, instead I am heavy
and awkward. When I want to be strong like a real
sword, instead I just sit here like a blackberry in a bowl
of yogurt. Once, I saw a suit of new skin floating
right in front of me. It was perfect. Just my size.
Sometimes, I spend the whole morning searching
for the morning. It was perfect. All I had to do
was step inside.

THE TOWN

The little town in my brain
has seen better days
but at least you're here,
you with the brown yarn hair,
you whose father farmed dairy.
The way you gaze at your palm
when you speak is sexy,
as if the brain was secondary
and our hands controlled us —
I wish that were true. Once
when we were together,
eating cheese by the river,
we watched the Gunderson dog
hunt down a hare.
He took its throat in
his teeth and thrashed.
By the time Ruth
Gunderson wrestled the dog off
the hare was dead, curled
in the grass like a towel.
You hid your face in your hands. Little
man that I was, I took this
as a chance to play the hero.
I'm sorry, I said, reaching across
the thin, peculiar air between us.
I'm sorry you had to see that,
letting my fingertips rest
on the skin of your back.
You said nothing, uncrossed
your legs and ran

toward the pine woods.
I just sat there
and watched ants feast
on the hare's blood, black
windmill in the distance spinning.

LITTLE CROWN

I was tossing a ball up and down while my mother

explained the series of events that led her to this town.

At one point, as a young girl, she had to wake up

each morning for a year and pretend to be herself.

At one point she found a drowned man in the creek

behind her parents' house. Even then, she understood life

was a test, so she placed a single cloudberry like a little

crown on the dead man's thumb, and never told

anyone what she had seen — until now, telling me.

I broke my favourite bowl tonight. I was standing
at the kitchen counter, scooping rice out
of a small pot, the rice so soft and white
with steam rising from it and dissolving like
forgetfulness. I spoke with Simone earlier.
Among the red leaves she looked so perfect
and bashful after she sneezed I forgot to say
Bless you, and she wriggled away, perturbed
by my failure to do what others do so naturally.
I wanted to tear my hair out, but I didn't
want strangers to think I was putting on a show,
so I just walked back to my apartment.
The bowl was baby blue with a floral pattern.
It was sitting on the countertop half-filled with rice
when I thought, *This is the end*. Like a farmer
shooting his sick goat in the head, I pushed
the bowl past the edge and watched it shatter.
Clumsy, I said, and stood there with a hand
cupped to my cheek while my roommates,
taking pity, cleaned up the rice and shards.
Once they were gone, the kitchen was still
and neat, like Simone's face when she is reading.
The appliances were in their proper places.
I studied my smile in the reflection of a spoon.
You're losing control, I said to the spoon.

ODE TO FLESH-EATING BACTERIA

Is there nothing
graceful, nothing
to be admired
in the way
the disease moved
from foot to
calf to mid-
thigh in the course
of a single night?
Is there nothing
lovely about
how the skin
purpled
as subcutaneous
tissue necrotized?
Is it not a little bit
religious when
a healthy cell
is overtaken
and gives itself
to a wholly new
and overwhelming
force? Was it
brave or just
stupid that I
wouldn't let myself
cry as I touched
the twitching
fingers of
the body the doctors

thought was going
to die? Is it wrong
to think maybe
the disease and
the surgeon
who sliced away at it
were not so
different, both
trying to finish
a job? There is
a version of events
in which the disease
wins, leaving
me stunned.
There is another
version of events
in which, years
later, black
locust branches
lean against
our telephone
wire, so my dad
climbs the ladder
and I hand him
a saw. It's summer.
He's wearing shorts.
For the first
time I see
the full scar,
like a long
crack in a plate.
*It's a funny kind
of tree*, he shouts

over the sound
of cutting.
It's got this real soft bark.

WHERE WILL YOU SPEND ETERNITY: HEAVEN OR HELL?

from a billboard on I-65 South

They say what nourishes us   also destroys us   like the dozen dried up

insects I found in a ring   around the light bulb   I envy them

for knowing what I don't   which is how to give love   freely without

saving some in an envelope tucked   in the back of my sock drawer

just in case   just in case I am never able to be honest with you

here are the facts of the situation as I see it   1) you are very pretty

2) there is a little kid inside of me   worrying you are too pretty

3) this world I have never been able   to hold at quite the right angle

4) my life means no more   than the lazy downswing of a Louisiana

cow's tail as we drive by it   5) this provides a kind of comfort

I went from a pain in the ass to a pretty word   you said that to me

in the car and no one else will know what it means   which maybe

makes me seem cryptic   but even that, I think — turning off the desire

to connect with a stranger   if it means remembering   you more clearly

— is a kind of heaven.

The charming man from Oklahoma
had sympathy for the shy boys of America.
It's not wrong to be quiet, he said, *but it is wrong to feel
silenced.* A semicircle of faces nodded.

The program the charming Oklahoman developed
also conveniently addressed the unstable
neighbourhood rabbit population.
It went like this:
— Hire a man with traps.
— Catch a bunch of rabbits.
— Rent a cabin in the woods.
— Bring a troop of shy boys.
— Release the rabbits.
— Have the boys hunt them.
— Kill as many as you can.
— Don't let the boys use guns.
— Teach them how to break necks with their hands.
— When night comes, collect the dead.
— If a boy wants to eat what he's killed, fine, cook it.
— If not, dispose of the bodies discreetly.
— Return the boys to their families.

The man was confident in his methods.
True, killing rabbits was not exactly admirable,
but neither was wasting your own life too nervous
to grab life properly. He explained this philosophy
— which he called *extreme exposure therapy* —
over dinner to his muscular teenage daughter,
who said *Cool* and chewed a chunk of potato.

The charming Oklahoman had no idea
he had just set a series of events in motion.
He couldn't have guessed how deep the need
in these boys went. He didn't know they would grow
dependent, seek out rabbits on their own to calm
their fraying nerves, strangle rabbits to steady
themselves before first dates. He didn't realize
that these shy boys would grow into shy
men with nine-to-fives and basements full of rabbits
to be killed casually, like heating up a little tea.

He did not expect an environmentalist
backlash. He did not imagine
that you would be standing
in a crowd on the lawn of town hall
in protest, wearing a summer dress.
People chanted, raised their signs, but all I
could do was sneak glances in your direction.
And think how smooth your skin looked.
And afterwards, I was brave for once —
I introduced myself, and you were kind.
We went out for veggie quesadillas.
We discussed rabbits, the language
of cruelty, what it means to suffer,

and soon enough we have a small apartment together.
We're raising a rabbit in the backyard.
We name her Amy. We feed her fresh hay,
buy her ironic toys. And as I watch you
put a slice of apple in her mouth, I sit
cross-legged in the grass, knowing what I know.
Knowing, for example, I am the worst thing
that could have possibly happened to you.

One night, I won't be able to hide it anymore.
I will break Amy's neck. I will cook her,
and eat her, and feel her blood moving
in my blood. I will lie down beside you
feeling that I am finally myself: calm, perfect.
Your summer dress hanging in the dark closet.
I will breathe on your neck and fall asleep.

In the morning, I will try to explain.
At first you will think I am kidding. Then
you will have a look on your face
I have never seen before.
There will be screaming.
You will tell me to leave.
Fucking right now just go.

So I will. And as I do
— even though I know
you cannot hear me — I will whisper
how sorry I am, and grateful for everything.

I was outside peeling the bark off a twig and counting down
from a thousand while everyone inside was committing adultery.

        The owls were black.

       The grass was black.

       The sky was saying   *sight*

      doesn't mean

              you aren't

      what you see. The creek

           agreed: *Yes,*

      we displace

           so little

      by being

      ourselves, no one

      can be sure   they are not

      what they most

              resist.

KEYS

The boy came to a clearing on the far side
of the forest. An abandoned piano sat in the frozen grass.
It was out of tune, but that was fine — he hardly knew
the difference. At first, he played some notes just to hear them,
nothing in particular. But soon he found himself
playing the curve of his father's belt. He played the way
his sister had looked down when she told him what
happened to her. He played what was left of his small
bag of almonds. All around him, bald trees slept.
His fingertips went numb. He played until he was no longer
playing, but was himself a key pressed by the weight
of the pale winter day he had chosen to wander into,
having reached the end of what he could explain.

LOVE POEM

I was hanging out inside
a shampoo bottle
when a messenger from the upper
world told me that you
were getting married. Sure is
a funny feeling — losing
what was never yours. So
at long last I decided
to get off my ass and start
the blog I had always
dreamt of, where I post
images of ants
carrying objects at least
twice the size of their own bodies.

I BUILT A PLAYGROUND

I built a playground where you can be alone,
like you like to be.

And I know how you like to play games
about time, so I built you

this special slide
that never ends —

you just keep sliding. Silly
how a life can move in one direction

for so long without turning.
I built you a doll

in case you don't feel like sliding. It
isn't beautiful, it

doesn't move, but I trained it to say
your favourite words — *stable,*

empty, yes — over and
over, yes, I think

it'll be fun. You can do
whatever you want: name it, hug it.

You could invite it into the slide,
but I guess that's a commitment

you'd probably rather skip. Probably rather
play the priest — so here, I got you this

ceremonial robe. Thought you'd like it. You're always talking
about spirits — here, it's exactly

what the real priests wear, I know
because I stole it

from a real church's closet.
It might be a little heavy

but I think you'll feel nice
strolling around in it, declaring

what is evil and what is good, what is ugly,
what is ugly. You can point to things

and say what they mean
and that's what they'll mean. Yes, the nifty part

of this playground is
you can never be wrong.

You can call the sky
the ground. You can fall off the tower

headfirst and be fine.
The woodchips you will land on

are soft — I paid for the softest woodchips.

My sister slips into her laceless shoes
and out the back door, entering the forest.
She arrives at a clearing and finds a dead boy
lying at the foot of a piano, two foxes
chewing on his face. Does she:

A. shoo the foxes away, call the police.
B. befriend the foxes, become a feral queen.
C. lie in the grass, pretend to be dead herself.
D. notice a cloud that resembles a brain.
E. notice a cloud that resembles a knife.
F. make a bracelet out of dandelion stems.
G. take some jujubes out of her pocket to eat.
H. attempt to play the cold keys, which stick.
I. take a selfie with the dead body #sleepingbeauty #foxy.
J. give the body a name, give the body a story.
K. lift the body up and dance with it slowly.
L. smell that its skin is turning yellow.

The architects hide in the branches, taking notes.

EGG TOSS

There once was a woman who was not
possible. She wished
she was, and complained to her friend, the fog.
Maybe you're not trying hard enough, the fog
said one night.
Okay, thought
the woman, now sitting in a diner
on a date with her mother.
She carried the world in her purse
like a small dog, took it out,
sprinkled salt in its oceans.
At first she felt euphoric,
then she needed more.
To wear a scarf that was a mirror,
to wear a scarf that was a mirror.
To climb ladders all alone in her garage.
I'll win the annual egg toss,
she thought, now sculpting
possibility. *I'll change my name
to Beatrice. I'll stand under an awning
in the downpour, and when the priest approaches
I will politely inform him
he has something stuck
in his teeth.*

PASTRY CONFERENCE

I was at this pastry conference
down in rural Tennessee,
and decided to take a shortcut
from the motel to the culinary college.
I walked through a patch of woods,
which was a sweet reprieve
from the extreme humidity.
I noticed several squirrels gathered
around the base of a dogwood tree.
They eyed me oddly.
It almost seemed as if they were preparing
to perform some masochistic ritual of sacrifice
in which one squirrel from the pack
is chosen at random
to be pinned to the tree,
legs pulled back, underbelly exposed,
while the others take turns
biting it, eating the heart,
absorbing — and eventually
digesting, evacuating — its bad luck,
thereby cleansing the pack
spiritually, allowing the squirrels
to live in peace
for another year.

On his way to church the boy
sees the church reflected
in the lake beside it with such
clarity it looks like a second,
identical church. *I'm sick
of our church. That one looks better,*
he says. His father tells him
to keep such silliness
to himself, but the boy
persists. *Let me go,* he says,
squirming free of his father's
rough hand. *Fine,* the father
says. *See what happens.*
So the boy jumps in and
sinks to the bottom. Sure
enough, there is a church there.
He walks in and notices
that everyone is soaked yet
they don't seem embarrassed.
This is the church for me,
he thinks. And it's great
for about five seconds. Then
he notices all of the faces
turning red — the parishioners
are drowning. Floating
in their pews, they are
praying for air. The boy screams
*Get out of here! You can breathe
outside!* He tries to drag
them out but they won't go.

There are hundreds of them,
fathers and sons, mothers
and an organ player. Bubbles rise
from the pastor's mouth. *It is
sort of beautiful*, the boy thinks
and, ignoring his own advice, dies
next to everyone else.

I was born in a place where all the people were clean,
where Joanie had no trouble falling asleep,
where Frank was allowed to pay for breakfast
using seashells he'd collected, where ten lizards
arranged themselves in a circle for no clear reason,
where nobody's wrists were too thin,
and when the man under the stars with a knife in his pants
examined his reflection in the lake and asked
Is this the night? Is this the night I finally sing?
his reflection replied *No, no, not tonight.*
So the man curled up in a ball and fell asleep
and dreamt of a place where all the people were dirty,
so dirty, they began to believe they were clean.

VIAL

I was having blood drawn again, undergoing testing
for my mysterious ailment. The phlebotomist and I
inhabited the usual mix of small talk and silence—
then she giggled. *What is it?* I said.   *It's just,
isn't this strange?* she said, holding up a vial of my blood.
To see what you are made of, in the hands of a stranger?
          Totally, I said. *I always thought that was weird,
but I never said anything because you're so professional.
You act like it's no big deal.*   *No, yeah,* she said,
gazing at the vial. *It's fucking wild. Your mom is in here,
your dad, your future kids. Your habits, your secrets.*
          I feel like your job is one of the realest jobs there is,
I said.   *All this for fourteen dollars an hour,* she said.
I wasn't sure what to say next. Money issues tend
to make me uncomfortable. *So,* she said, *you want
to party?* She peeled off her gloves, hit the lights,
uncapped the vial containing my blood, and took a sip.
The needle was still in my arm, but the hose
was disconnected so my blood dripped onto the floor.
She grabbed the hose, put it to my lip. *Try some,*
she said.   *No, no,* I said. *It was great to meet you, but—*
          Listen, she said. *I know your type. I've tasted you.
Just do what I say, you dirty dog. Take this terrible dream
out of my head. Take this terrible dream, and suck on it.*

When I was a child, I stepped on a snail. I was playing this game where I walked back and forth across the lawn, back and forth between my mother and father, kiss mother on the cheek, father on the forehead—I was walking toward father when I stepped on the snail. I felt it crunch and looked and saw the mess. I didn't want them to see. The only option that made sense was to swallow it whole, so I picked it up and put it in my mouth. But of course they saw, and lunged, and pulled the snail out. We stopped playing that game.

Raindrops assisted in my sexual awakening. After a storm, I'd sneak out to the woods behind the house. I'd see drops dangling off branches, off tips of leaves, pooling in the crevice of a stone. And I would lick, lick. I was expressing myself as a deer. One time I got sick after licking. I vomited for twenty hours. I think a piece of my intestine came out with the vomit.

A woman approached me on the street and told me to stick out my tongue. I was a teenager, still unsure what normal meant, and this was New York City, so I did as I was told. She took my tongue between her teeth and bit down. We both kept our eyes open. I think this fact amazed her, and in her amazement she bit harder. She let go only when the blood started.

Afterwards, she bought me an espresso and told me her name. She said she did what she did because of what someone else had done. And she wasn't sorry, exactly, but felt the need to explain.

BOBCAT

walking through the woods / at
midnight / we were headed for the
lake / where we / would skinny-dip
when two yellow eyes / appeared
on the path / we froze / they didn't
blink / there was something tense
in their stillness / you said it was
probably a bobcat / maybe let's not
so / we didn't / we turned back and
shared a bed / untouching / as usual
you fell / asleep first and I wondered
what kept us apart / those nights
our ritual / awkwardness / I thought
of the animal / who blocked our path
and could see her now / for what
she was / a hostess / welcoming us
to a land of risk / cold lake water
to hold our nakedness / the animal
asked / are you ready / I wanted
to shake you awake / bring you back

to the animal and say / confidently
yes / table for two / but instead
I just lay there / in the perfect / quiet
country / darkness / and imagined
the outline of your chest / rising and
falling / rising / and falling as you
slept

THIRD DATE

We watched a yellow butterfly bounce, bounce,
then get annihilated by a truck, which cast a wing-sized shadow
over our trip to the state park. It was there, under the sugar
maple canopy, darling, that I learned of your hypoglycemia.
All I had packed were two apples and some nuts.
We got rained on, which made the landscape
a bit muddy, but also greener —
a beauty we trudged through
like two lost soldiers.
Our camp had come under fire. We'd been forced to flee.
All I had to drink was half a canteen
of dirty water — you carried the knife. As we moved
nervously through the forest, you told stories.
My friend back home is a chess master, but he won't play with me.
He thinks it'll affect our friendship.
                              I worked as a model
for a gardening magazine even though I'm allergic
to leafy greens. I listened madly. Listening
felt like the difference between nothingness and maple trees,
and since all you needed was a pair of ears, you allowed me
to follow you even after we escaped.
In your apartment, you were the queen
cutting meat with a butterfly knife, queen who spoke
through a mouthful of grapes.
I was the soldier who forgot his own name. I was the soldier
you declared a king. I was a boy wearing a crown
made of string.

PORTRAIT, WARTIME

Although I barely speak
his language, I persuade him
to wear his finest shirt
and carry his favourite toy
(a knife in an elkskin sheath).
When I explain what it means
to be photographed,
I notice a hint of pride
crossing his face, if it is possible
to feel pride after watching
your mother be taken.
I aim for his heart.
Are you ready? 1, 2 —

instead of film,
lead. Instead of an opening
to allow light in, the light
receives a visitor.

THE FALL

The boy was walking along
a mountain's ledge
when, startled
by the cry of a hawk, he fell off.
In an effort to fit a lifetime
into seven seconds, the boy fell in
and out of love several times
while falling.
He fell in love with the fissures
in the rock face,
but then decided this love
was merely aesthetic.
He fell in love with the speed
at which he was falling,
then decided this love
was too abstract.
He fell in love with the rubble
he was fast approaching,
but this love began
to seem morbid.
Finally, he fell in love with the hawk—
in love with the hawk's cry,
how it arrived so suddenly.
He fell in love with his own
nervousness,
which had caused him to trip.
These versions of love felt
decent to him, so he decided
to hold onto them,
to carry them

into the afterlife.
Of course, there was no afterlife
at the end of the fall, though — just
some sun-warmed stones.

THERE GO GORDON'S GOATS

past the house where his marriage ended,
past the guitar unplayed in the basement,
past the farm with orange trees,
past the ash of a dog he put to sleep,
past the son who wears a book for a face,
past the disease we do not talk about,
past the midnight kitchen where he chews
tortilla chips and philosophy,
past the furthest forest he can name,
the goats finally arrive at a clearing
where they are greeted by his mother,
who has no memory
and scratches their hairy chins and tells a story
about her son who went to the store to buy milk,
her son who will be back any minute now.

They say to document the conditions now because

soon the fading will begin. What the fading is

I do not know, so let me begin by telling you

about the cold. When you wish to eat with a spoon,

it must be warmed next to the fire first

or it sticks to your lips. When my daughter went

missing, I knew it was because she was black-haired

and beautiful, and these are the traits the souls

who live between stones find attractive, and so

she was taken. When you wash your hair it freezes,

and when you brush it beside the fire the water

falls from the comb in the form of snow.

The winter months are not as dark as you might think,

despite the absent sun. Some of us carry on

conversations with juniper trees. But before

I go too far, let me say that our children do read

the Bible — and no, we don't eat with dirty hands,

as some have suggested. When the male bear slept

with the human woman, the child emerged with the body

of a bear but the face of a human. No choice but to kill it.

When my daughter was born, she was given

a piece of boiled reindeer fat to suck on. Sugar

had not come to us yet. Now that I am alone,

I can spend all day watching reindeer eat lichen,

their quiet chewing entrancing me until I am both

here and not here. It is commonly known the wolf

was invented by the devil, and if you are not careful

your snow will turn red while you sleep.

I do not think I could live without my reindeer.

Like them, I prefer circles to squares.

I know we exist in a middle world —

there are spirits below you can touch

by passing through a hole at the bottom

of a lake with the help of certain fish.

But sometimes I wonder what would happen

if there were no other worlds, just this one.

What the fading would mean then.

I suppose it makes no difference. Either way,

I keep packing grass in my shoes for warmth.

The sky had a purple slant to it this morning.

It is said that whoever flies before his wings can bear him

lands in a dunghill, so I have told you this story carefully.

The shot was fired in the 1800s,
in Holland, in the woods to the north.
Elsa the grandmother was out gathering
mushrooms. For twenty years
she'd been foraging there,
and the woods were pretty much
as they had always been, just a little bit
more noise around the edges.
There was a spruce tree
Elsa liked to sit at the base of
and feel small. On the afternoon
of the accident, she had fallen asleep slumped
at the foot of that spruce,
mushroom basket by her side.
In her final dream, Elsa is trying to describe
her first kiss, while a semicircle of people
eagerly await the details.
She is trying to tell her story, but she is afraid
of offending these people, people
who don't know how lips feel
because they don't have mouths.

THE CRITIC FALLS IN LOVE

Why were people so impressed
that flower petals resembled vaginas?
I said, making an argument
about modern art, about which
I know next to nothing.
Nature is always mirroring
itself back at itself, I said,
coyly sipping cider.
Hours later, walking home
alone in the warm spring air,
I watched a black cat
crossing the street nearly
get hit by a white Ford Escape.
A pack of drunken women
discussing horses staggered
by me on the sidewalk.
Life was becoming
dangerously symbolic.
The wind undid my shoelaces.
An elm tree I once trusted
pinned me to the sidewalk.
I wanted to scream *OK! OK!*
I've learned my lesson! But
then I saw them: flowers
with thin green bodies
and pink faces snaking toward me.
One by one, they slid in my mouth.
I could no longer think.
I was gagging. The procession
was accompanied by a low chant.

Nature, nature, nature,
nature, nature, nature,
they whispered while travelling
the length of my tongue.
Nature, nature, nature,
they piled up in my stomach.
Nature, nature, until I
was the one saying it.

INTIMACY

Interior. Living Room. 5 a.m. I read while she sleeps.

In theory, I would like to tell you everything.

Instead, I play these language games.

Inability to relax around those you love most —

what do you call that? Incredible to be unable

to speak of it except in riddles. (Thank you,

riddles.) Inseparable, I sometimes think:

my self from the shelter it has built.

In here! I'm down here! Drop a worm

on a string — I'll bite. Indecent,

I know, to perform this way for you.

In pursuit of honesty, I create a lot of steam.

In case you were wondering, that thing from before —

it didn't work out. Innkeeper seeks

new inn to keep, intricate defence

mechanisms preferred. So introduce me

to your friends: I promise to wear my best face.

After the lasers and scissors and needles and pills,
men need somewhere to go, a place to feel safe
and temporarily normal before reentering
society radically beautiful. It is a kind of hotel,
full of natural light, and nobody is supposed to feel
ashamed of their scars. Of course we are ashamed anyway,
but it's also a time of excitement as we watch
our bodies realize their ideal shapes, our wounds
gradually heal, our new hair grow. There are several
exotic plants which the Surgeon recommends
we contemplate re: not getting trapped inside
a static conception of beauty. My favourite
is the prickly orange one whose flesh somewhat
resembles my post-op scalp. All in all,
things are going well, except that my friend Max
is fully recovered, so he's leaving. We used to stay up
late watching crime dramas. We both had nightmares
about being chased by giant insects. *Don't worry,*
he said. *Once you get out, we'll go out for drinks.*
We'll just be two guys with perfect jawlines and balls
that hang symmetrically. This was a relief to hear
because I'd been scared Max wouldn't want
to be friends anymore in the outer world.
You're led to believe these ideas growing up, like beauty
changes people—but that doesn't have to be true.
When I get out of here, I'm gonna take
that prickly plant with me, so I never forget.
When I get out of here, I'm gonna take a taxi
straight to my father's grave. Curl up beside
it and sleep.

GAME

The winner skins
the loser and wears
their skin as a delicate
garment to the annual
gala.

The loser spends
the rest of their skinless
life folding paper
airplanes out of photographs
of the winner.

SUPERSTAR

I was standing in the dust
in the centre of a stadium,
a crowd of thousands
watching from the stands.
Some took photographs,
some ate snacks,
some used their arms to gesture
at me indecipherably.
I was alone in the centre
of the stadium,
standing in a field of dust.
Objects were arranged
in my vicinity.
I walked over to a dresser
and opened each drawer.
Each drawer was empty
except for the bottom one,
which contained
a hairbrush. I brushed
my short, thin hair with it.
The audience applauded.
There was a bowl filled
with milk resting on a mattress.
I dipped my hand into the bowl—
the audience gasped.
Gasped as if witnessing death.
I took my hand out of the bowl.
The audience screamed
and moaned, parents shielding
their children's faces.

I wanted everyone to know
I was okay. I poured the milk
into the dust, creating
a kind of mud.
I knelt down and rolled
around in it. *Look, look,*
I am a pig, funny,
everyone should stop crying now.
It was then with horror
I recalled our milk was sacred.
I could have touched
any other object.
I could have broken in half
the hairbrush, the abacus.
I could have urinated
on the mattress,
torn up the orange peels.
But not — never — the milk.
The Gamemaster was approaching
with a large pair of scissors.
I stared at my trembling
milky fingers and told them
I loved them. *This is not*
your fault, I said.
I said, *When that blade comes down…*
When that blade comes down…
I couldn't think what to say next.
The Gamemaster was very
very close now. I said,
When that blade comes down…

The prison was a tower by the sea. The tower was a used contact lens left behind on my sink. The prison was a memory I could not stop scratching. The tower was free to enter but you had to pay to go up. The sea was there for you when you needed something to spit into. The sea had feelings once, but then a man in a tuxedo whispered to the sea that no, you should not have feelings, that makes it awkward. The sea apologized, said she wouldn't do it again. After that she just crashed and crashed — no one knew what she was thinking. I watched from the top of the tower, foaming at the mouth. The tuxedo man poked me with a whale's rib bone, insisting that I sing, sing along to the crashing of the sea. Lyrics tumbled down the teleprompter. And I would have gladly sold my voice, but I couldn't read the words on the screen. My crime was a silence, I have no doubt about this. Tomorrow I will spit into the sea again.

The art museum is empty except for one woman. No employees around to check her ticket, make her pay for an ice cream sandwich, or stop her from running her cold fingers over the paintings. While she walks through a hall of white faces, sirens sound in the distance, gunshots reduced to applause and drowned out by the echo of her footsteps. In the Modern Wing, a video shows two men playing chess with live beetles. Every time a man moves a beetle to a spot, the beetle just moves somewhere else. She licks the chocolate off her fingertips, takes out an index card, writes *2017.* Behind her, a neon sign reads *Everything You Can Imagine Is Real.* She curls up on the tile and sleeps for six thousand years.

THE MASSES

In the department store,
a corner has been designated
the Play Area for kids.
Most swim
in a colourful ball pit, but one
is off to the side.
I notice he is reading
The Art of War.
When he sees me
seeing him, he starts to cry.
What's wrong? I ask.
Ugh, he says, *the masses*.
It's been a while since
I let the masses get me down,
but here in the Play Area
I give myself permission.
I know, I know, I say,
and we sit there bitterly
watching bargain hunters
come and go.
Don't you hate cats, too?
he asks. Personally,
I like cats, but I don't
want to spoil the mood.
Sure. Hate them, I say.
The kid grins.
Then you're going to love this.
He pulls the skinned
corpse of a cat
out of his knapsack.

The eyes have been pulled out
and stuffed in the mouth.

I was playing some putt-putt golf all by myself, no big deal,
just a Wednesday afternoon in the middle of summer.
I was two holes in when my pocket vibrated, a call
from a number I didn't recognize. The voice on the other side
said I was needed at the hospital ASAP. *Sure, sure, I'll come by*
this evening, I said to the voice. *Sir, your mother is not well.*
We need you to sign a form before we can proceed, it said.
Understood, I said. *A dreadful situation. I'll sign the form*
right after I finish putting my way through this course. I hung up.
I was trying to suss out the proper angle on hole seven
when my pocket began vibrating again. This time it was Liz.
We were supposed to be *making the most* out of our last
few days together. I didn't answer. I was lining up a putt
from five feet away, trying to account for the very real
possibility of falling into the sand trap if I overshot.
In a quiet neighbourhood of my brain, a memory of Liz played.
We'd been sitting on a swing in her mother's backyard.
Liz made a joke, and instead of laughing I accidentally
said *I love you.* It slipped out — my first time saying that
to anyone and meaning it. *Sorry,* I said. *Don't be sorry,*
she said, *that's just weirder.* When I didn't pick up her call,
she texted me a question mark, so I texted back *Sry,*
unexpected work thing came up. I was staring at the blades
of the windmill guarding the hole I was supposed to putt
my ball through. As they spun and spun, I thought
to myself: *How safe, how perfect. Let me stand here and just stare*
at this circle forever. Let me hold this club, but never use it.
Let the ball sit on the green for so long it forgets what it means
to be touched. Let the touch of that forgetting be enough.

THE HOLE

In the dark, you say
We all have a hole
we're trying to fill.
We fill it
with different things:
television, infidelity,
whatever.   I say
I don't think
I have a hole.
I have a boy
who sits on a tree stump
telling stories.
All night
he fires his pistol
blindly into the sky.
Every once in a while
he hits an owl as it
flies by.
He describes
the strangeness
that falls, holding it up
to the light—but
it is dark, and you
have already
fallen asleep.

Bless the men with holes in them, and bless the women.
Bless eight uninterrupted hours of television.
The man cried while the woman laughed
then the man laughed while the woman cried—
they wanted to line up, but didn't.
Bless the tattered net hanging from the orange
metal rim. The thin kid shooting baskets. The cat
who lets the spider live. The construction
worker who drops a brick on his foot, which stings
but he just laughs. Bless that laugh as it evaporates.
And I think I could spend the next twenty years getting high with you
on the hillside by the airport, getting high and watching planes take off
and land, and land, and take off.

THE MACHINE

The machine can sense when you are afraid
so try to control your fear
when you're near the machine.

Don't fall in love
with me, he said.

Certain mistakes possess
a glamour before you
make them, and then
after, they still
shimmer a bit.

The way blowing
on his eyelashes
made her feel
like the wind.

BUTTERFLY HUNTER

I had a date with the butterfly hunter, who was rumoured
to have discovered a new species.

Watch, he said,
placing the blade

in his mouth.
He made a clean cut

of his cheek,
which flapped

open, bleeding —
a simple red wing.

CANNONBALL

I heard it was my turn to be shot from the cannon. At first
I didn't believe it. People are always joking about such things.
My friends told me it was serious this time, though. Apparently
there was a meeting about it, and people were divided on the issue.
Then an old man took the microphone. No one had seen him in years,
but he showed up to this meeting because he felt strongly
that I should be shot from the cannon. His speech was so
eloquent, apparently, that certain members of the audience wept.
He argued that we were facing the most challenging moment
in human history, and the cannon stood for human resilience,
and I stood for all humans. By launching me from the cannon
they were launching themselves up too. I was simply the spokesperson.
And what an honour that was, getting to carry the weight of the whole
human family on my skinny shoulders. *Fuck*, I thought to myself.
I had long suspected metaphors would be my downfall.
I'm flattered, I told my friend Amy. *But why do I have to be
shot from the cannon, specifically? Couldn't I just, I don't know,
do some community service? Or maybe give a speech of my own?*
I am quite nervous about public speaking, so you can tell
this was serious to me. No one who had been shot from the cannon
had returned to say how it went. *But don't worry*, Amy said.
*There's probably a place over the hill that's better than this shitty town.
That's probably where you're going. Plus*, she said, *I hear the air is like
a blanket when you're in it. People are so afraid of falling, they don't
enjoy the flying, but the truth is they're the same* . . . *Wow*, I said,
somewhat offended that Amy had used my impending doom
to generalize about fear and pleasure. I didn't have time for that.
Still, it seemed the world had made up its mind, so I started walking —
I was turning myself in. Every time I passed a car, I thought
to myself, *I love you car, this is the end*. And when I approached

the receptionist at town hall, she was licking her lips, seductively
I thought, although they may have been just chapped.
I cleared my throat. *I'm ready*, I said. She looked up at me.
Suddenly I regretted everything. I leaned in. Gave her a small hug.
Oh, she said. *Well, alright. I'll tell my boss to order a cannon.*
We didn't think you would actually come.

ACKNOWLEDGEMENTS

Thank you to the editors of the following publications, where poems from this book first appeared: *Arkansas International, Best New Poets 2013, BOAAT, Boiler Journal, Colorado Review, DIAGRAM, Field, Forklift Ohio, Gulf Coast, Hobart, Iowa Review, Juked, Kenyon Review, Lemon Hound, Maisonneuve, Massachusetts Review, Nashville Review, New Ohio Review, The Pinch, Pleiades, Sixth Finch, Sycamore Review, West Branch.*

Thank you to the organizations who supported the writing of these poems: Canada Council for the Arts, House of Anansi Press, Huazhong Agricultural University, MacDowell Colony, Ohio State University, PEN Canada, RBC Emerging Artists Project, Sewanee Writers' Conference, Vassar College, Vermont Studio Center, Yaddo.

Thank you to Ji Yeo, whose photography project "Beauty Recovery Room" inspired my poem of the same title.

Thank you to this amazing string of teachers I have followed: Archy LaSalle, Debi Milligan, Jennifer Hogue, Mike Young, Ronald Sharp, Amitava Kumar, Michael Joyce, Beth Darlington, Paul Kane, Henri Cole, Andrew Hudgins, Maggie Smith, Kathy Fagan.

Thank you to the many people whose hands are in these poems: Shelley Wong, Janelle DolRayne, David Winter, Raena Shirali, Megan Peak, Lauren Cook, Willie VerSteeg, Paige Quiñones, Cait Weiss, Graham Barnhart, Dan O'Brien, Chris Morris, Jessica Lieberman, Margaret Cipriano, Rachel Chait, Florence Wallis, Melanie Risch, Sofi Thanhauser, Peter Hoover, Elizabeth Ditmanson, Nick Amphlett, Edgar Kunz, Mary Ruefle, Ashley Yang-Thompson.

Thank you to Jake Bauer for reading a thousand drafts. Thank you to Andrew Battershill and Suzannah Showler for pointing me in the right direction. Thank you to Kevin Connolly for accepting this book and improving it.

This book is dedicated to my friends and family. And particular animals along the way.

Author photograph: Maija Harvey

Mikko Harvey received the 2017 RBC/PEN Canada New Voices Award, and his poems appear in places such as *Iowa Review, Kenyon Review, Lemon Hound,* and *Maisonneuve*. He attended Vassar College and Ohio State University, and he is currently an associate poetry editor for *Fairy Tale Review*. This is his first book.